LIBRARY SMARTS

EXPLORE THE LIBRARY

JANET PIEHL

Lerner Publications Company • Minneapolis

For my favorite library workers, Luciano Ward and Ann Piehl

Lerner Publications Company
A division of Lerner Publishing Group, Inc.
241 First Avenue North
Minneapolis, MN 55401 U.S.A.

Website address: www.lernerbooks.com

Library of Congress Cataloging-in-Publication Data

Piehl, Janet.
    Explore the library / by Janet Piehl.
        pages   cm. — (Library smarts)
    Includes index.
    ISBN 978–1–4677–1500–3 (lib. bdg. : alk. paper)
    ISBN 978–1–4677–1750–2 (eBook)
    1. Libraries—Juvenile literature. 2. Librarians—Juvenile literature.
    I. Title.
    Z665.5P54 2014
    027—dc23   2013004388

Manufactured in the United States of America
1 – CG – 7/15/13

TABLE OF CONTENTS

The Library

Welcome to the library! A library is a place to read, learn, and have fun. You can borrow books, music, movies, and more from the library.

Let's explore the library!

People go to the library to read. They look for books. They do homework. They use computers. They play with their friends.

Children, teenagers, and adults all go to the library. Libraries are for everyone!

Librarians

Librarians work in libraries. They help people find answers to questions.

Where are the dog books? Which book is right for me? May I use a computer? Where is the bathroom? A librarian can answer all of these questions.

Finding Books

Do you need to find a book? Ask a librarian for help. She takes you to a computer. A tool called a **library catalog** is on the computer.

Type in the title of the book. The library catalog tells you about the book. The catalog gives you the book's **call number**. The call number says where the book is in the library. The number is like the book's address in the library.

Child's
QP
301
.J588
2013

Call number

Write down the call number. The librarian will show you to the book. Look at the call number from the library catalog. Look at the call number on the book. Do they match?

Open the book. Try to read the first page. The librarian can help you decide if the book is just right for you.

Libraries have all kinds of books. They have books to read with an adult and books to read on your own. They have books with made-up stories and books with true stories.

Libraries have books to read for fun. They have books to read for homework. They have books for children, teenagers, and adults.

Story Time

Families come to the library for **story time**. Librarians, children, and adults read books, sing songs, and play games together.

Older children talk about books. Some make art projects. Others play video games. Everyone can have fun at the library!

Checking Out Books

It is time to check out your books. Checking out books is free. But you must return the books after a few weeks. Do you have a **library card**? A library card lets you borrow books, music, movies, and more. It shows the name of your library. It shows your name and a special number.

A library worker scans your library card. She scans the books. She gives the books back to you. She tells you to return them by their **due date**.

A library card

Returning Books

People return books in a drop box. Then library workers collect the books. Workers put the books back on the shelves. They make sure the books go in the right places.

Soon someone else explores the library. He asks a librarian. The librarian helps him find a book. He checks it out and promises to return it. Best of all, he reads the book!

GLOSSARY

call number: a number that tells where a book can be found in a library. A call number is like a book's address in the library.

due date: the day by which library books must be returned. People can borrow library books for a few weeks. Then they must return them.

librarians: people who are specially trained to work in a library. Librarians answer questions and help people find what they are looking for in the library.

library card: a card that lets people borrow books, music, movies, and more from a library. You can get your own library card at your local library.

library catalog: a library computer tool that tells facts about books. It says where books can be found in the library.

story time: a library program where a librarian reads books, sings songs, and plays games with children and sometimes adults. It is a time for children to start to learn to read.

INDEX

Photo acknowledgments: The images in this book are used with the permission of: © Marta Johnson/Independent Picture Service, p. 5; © Todd Strand/Independent Picture Service, pp. 7, 11 (upper left), 19 (lower right); © Robert Kneschke/Dreamstime.com, p. 9; © Rmarmion/Dreamstime.com, p. 11; © Comstock Images, p. 13; © Lucidio Studio Inc/First Light/Getty Images, p. 15; © iStockphoto.com/Jani Bryson, p. 17; © SW Productions/Photodisc/Getty Images, p. 19; © iStockphoto.com/Brad Killer, p. 21; © iStockphoto.com/Steve Debenport, p. 23.

Front cover: © Rmarmion/Dreamstime.com.

Main body text set in Gill Sans Infant Std Regular 18/22. Typeface provided by Monotype Typography.